JAMES GARFIELD

The Presidents of the United States

George Washington
1789–1797

John Adams
1797–1801

Thomas Jefferson
1801–1809

James Madison
1809–1817

James Monroe
1817–1825

John Quincy Adams
1825–1829

Andrew Jackson
1829–1837

Martin Van Buren
1837–1841

William Henry Harrison
1841

John Tyler
1841–1845

James Polk
1845–1849

Zachary Taylor
1849–1850

Millard Fillmore
1850–1853

Franklin Pierce
1853–1857

James Buchanan
1857–1861

Abraham Lincoln
1861–1865

Andrew Johnson
1865–1869

Ulysses S. Grant
1869–1877

Rutherford B. Hayes
1877–1881

James Garfield
1881

Chester Arthur
1881–1885

Grover Cleveland
1885–1889

Benjamin Harrison
1889–1893

Grover Cleveland
1893–1897

William McKinley
1897–1901

Theodore Roosevelt
1901–1909

William H. Taft
1909–1913

Woodrow Wilson
1913–1921

Warren Harding
1921–1923

Calvin Coolidge
1923–1929

Herbert Hoover
1929–1933

Franklin D. Roosevelt
1933–1945

Harry Truman
1945–1953

Dwight Eisenhower
1953–1961

John F. Kennedy
1961–1963

Lyndon B. Johnson
1963–1969

Richard Nixon
1969–1974

Gerald Ford
1974–1977

Jimmy Carter
1977–1981

Ronald Reagan
1981–1989

George H. W. Bush
1989–1993

William J. Clinton
1993–2001

George W. Bush
2001–2009

Barack Obama
2009–

★ ★ ★ ★ ★ ★ ★ ★ ★ ★ ★ ★ ★ ★ ★ ★ ★ ★ ★

JAMES GARFIELD

WIL MARA

 **Marshall Cavendish**
Benchmark
New York

Other Marshall Cavendish Offices:
Marshall Cavendish International (Asia) Private Limited, 1 New Industrial Road, Singapore 536196 • Marshall Cavendish International (Thailand) Co Ltd. 253 Asoke, 12th Flr, Sukhumvit 21 Road, Klongtoey Nua, Wattana, Bangkok 10110, Thailand • Marshall Cavendish (Malaysia) Sdn Bhd, Times Subang, Lot 46, Subang Hi-Tech Industrial Park, Batu Tiga, 40000 Shah Alam, Selangor Darul Ehsan, Malaysia

Marshall Cavendish is a trademark of Times Publishing Limited

All websites were available and accurate when this book was sent to press.

Library of Congress Cataloging-in-Publication Data

Mara, Wil.
James Garfield / Wil Mara.
p. cm. — (Presidents and their times)
Summary: Provides comprehensive information on President James Garfield and places him within his historical and cultural context. Also explored are the formative events of his times and how he responded.
Includes bibliographical references and index.
ISBN 978-1-60870-183-4 — ISBN 978-1-60870-725-6 (ebook)
1. Garfield, James A. (James Abram), 1831–1881—Juvenile literature. 2. Presidents—United States—Biography—Juvenile literature. I. Title. II. Series.
E687.M37 2012
973.8'4092—dc22'
[B]
2010039864

Editor: Christine Florie
Publisher: Michelle Bisson
Art Director: Anahid Hamparian
Series Designer: Alex Ferrari

Photo research by Marybeth Kavanagh

Cover photo by Calvin Curtis/Private Collection/ Peter Newark American Pictures/ The Bridgeman Art Library

The photographs in this book are used by permission and through the courtesy of: *SuperStock*: 45; Science Faction, 3, 24, 81, 82; Everett Collection, 6, 74; *Getty Images*: MPI, 9, 26, 33; Kean Collection, 18; James Fitz Ryder/George Eastman House, 23; Buyenlarge, 40, 64; Hulton Archive, 43, 71, 72; Library of Congress, 49; *North Wind Picture Archives*: 10, 15, 50, 56, 59, 66, 70, 82L; *The Bridgeman Art Library*: Henry Herbert/Ferens Art Gallery, Hull Museums, UK, 11; *Corbis*: 14; Bettmann, 61; *The Image Works*: Photo12, 12; Mary Evans Picture Library, 53; *Everett Collection, Inc.*: 28; *Alamy*: North Wind Picture Archives, 31; *Library of Congress*: 35, 63, 83L, 83R; *Newscom*: Picture History, 77, 79

Printed in Malaysia
1 3 5 6 4 2

CONTENTS

Born a poor farm boy, James Garfield nevertheless gained an extensive education, served in the Civil War, earned a seat in the House of Representatives, and was elected the twentieth president of the United States.

EARLY YEARS IN OHIO *One*

*J*ames Garfield started life as a poor farm boy and eventually became the twentieth president of the United States. He was a highly ambitious individual, and he had strong speaking skills as well as the gifts of charm and persuasion. He read widely and went to great lengths to educate himself on any subject that interested him. In his youth he impressed his teachers with his love of learning, and his classmates with his outgoing and cheerful personality.

After graduating from college, Garfield accepted a teaching position and within a year was made the school's president. Soon after, his interest in politics began to blossom, and he was elected to the Ohio State Senate in 1859. His sense of duty led him to take part in one of the greatest conflicts in American history, the Civil War (1861–1865). When his participation in the Civil War began, he was given the rank of colonel and the command of a small group of volunteers. He fought in several battles without sustaining serious injury, and by the time he finished his military service in December 1863, he was a two-star general.

Garfield's war record made him a hero back home, and he used this reputation to forward his growing interest in politics. In 1862, while he was still in the Union army, he was elected to the U.S. House of Representatives. This victory put him at the heart of power in America. As a member of the radical faction of the newly formed **Republican Party**, he often found himself at odds

7

with the party's leader and the nation's president, Abraham Lincoln. His occasional opposition to Lincoln's policies sometimes had a damaging effect on Garfield's popularity with voters. Nevertheless, he often felt he had to speak his mind on key issues, even at the risk of harming his political career. He took part in the Reconstruction era following the war and in time became one of Ohio's favorite sons. He was reelected to his congressional seat time and time again.

Garfield reached the presidency by chance; his name was not on the original ballot at the Republican nominating convention in 1880. However, endless bickering among Republican delegates over the original nominees led them to pick Garfield as a compromise candidate, partially out of fear that the American voters would turn away from the Republican Party if it appeared too divided. Garfield gratefully accepted his party's support, and in the general election, he beat his Democratic opponent by a razor-thin margin. Nevertheless, he had achieved a nearly impossible dream. The poor farm boy from Ohio had reached the highest office in the land. It must have seemed too good to be true.

BIRTH AND BOYHOOD

James Abram Garfield was born November 19, 1831, in a tiny Ohio township known simply as Orange. Located a few miles southeast of Cleveland, Orange was part of a larger section of Ohio known as the Western Reserve. Parts of the Reserve were still a wild and wooded frontier area, largely untouched by the white settlers moving across the American West. Garfield was the last U.S. president to be born in a log cabin. James's father, Abram, was a farmer; his mother, Eliza (née Ballou), kept house

James Garfield was born and raised in a log cabin in the Ohio township of Orange.

and raised the couple's four children (a fifth died at an early age). James, the youngest, had two sisters and a brother.

Before James was two years old, Abram, usually a healthy and able man, died of a respiratory illness. The future suddenly looked bleak for the Garfield family. They had a fair amount of debt, and suddenly they were without the person who had been doing the grueling farmwork. They had about thirty acres, plus their modest cabin. Under such circumstances, a widow would often sell the property and take her children elsewhere, perhaps to move in with a relative. However, James's father had managed his farm shrewdly and efficiently, and Eliza, in spite of her grief, had every intention of doing the same.

Eliza Garfield raised her children on her own after the death of her husband, Abram.

Eliza Garfield was energetic and hardworking, and she had a deep sense of right and wrong. She tolerated no misbehavior in the household and punished her children for everything from using foul language to laziness. She taught them the importance of self-discipline and of using their time wisely. She was a member of a religious denomination known as the Disciples of Christ, and she frequently read the Bible to her children at night. James became so familiar with Bible passages that he could quote many from memory. He sometimes tested his friends on their knowledge of the Bible and scolded them if they made mistakes. Eliza's influence on her youngest son was profound, and they remained close throughout his life.

James grew into a strong and healthy boy, and he seemed to enjoy farmwork. When he was still too small to take on more strenuous tasks, he herded the animals, turned the soil to ready it for planting, carried wood and built fires, and took care of minor house repairs. He was not a natural farmer like his father, but, driven by an ambitious nature that would serve him throughout his life, he always put in a full day of work and made sure his duties were completed. As one of his early biographers wrote, "He was not an enthusiastic farmer, but he was an enthusiastic helper of his mother; and from the time he was able—he was always willing—he shouldered his full share of all the farm-work, finding his special province in the lighter labors of seed-time and harvest, and, in the Fall, in 'chores' about the barn-house, until the Winter's snowy mantle covered the ground."

One of the most significant social movements on the rise during Garfield's youth was the antislavery movement known as **abolitionism**. It was fueled in part by an increase in Christian **evangelism**. In truth, anyone who believed that slavery was inherently immoral and an offense to basic human rights, Christian or not, was considered a follower of abolitionist thought. Although the abolition movement was not new, it began gathering its greatest force during the first half of the 1800s.

Young James helped with chores around the farm.

Slavery

Slavery in the United States began in the early 1600s, when Africans were brought to Virginia to work as farmhands. These people were sold to and owned outright by plantation owners—an arrangement called chattel slavery. A slave could not attain freedom unless his or her owner declared it so, and the individual was, as such, regarded as property. Freed slaves often found it difficult to gain solid footing or advancement in society, as they were considered by many to be inferior to white people in spite of their newfound freedom. Some slaves sought revenge on their former masters after they became free. They sometimes formed mobs and committed acts of violence ranging from property damage to physical abuse and even murder.

A situation similar in certain ways to slavery—one largely confined to whites—was indentured servitude, where, in exchange for transportation from Europe, food, clothing, and lodging, workers were obligated to remain in the service of a master for a certain number of years before gaining their freedom.

In the northern states, male slaves often worked as craftsmen and female slaves as housekeepers, whereas in the southern states, the majority of slaves did farmwork. On plantations, slave labor was crucial to profitability, with the great majority of slaves receiving food and shelter but no pay. By the opening of the nineteenth century, slaves constituted about one-sixth of the overall U.S. population. They were concentrated in the most agrarian areas, with the greatest numbers in Virginia, the Carolinas, and Maryland.

With abolitionist sentiment spreading throughout the northern states, slavery there dwindled. In Garfield's native state of Ohio, slavery had been banned long before he was born. There were no slaves working on his family's small farm, and young James saw little firsthand evidence of its existence.

In the South, however, slavery was a fact of life. With the invention of Eli Whitney's cotton gin in 1793 and the subsequent establishment of new cotton plantations, there came the need for even more slave labor. During this time the contrast between northern and southern states became more pronounced than ever. By 1830 the United States was home to more than 2 million slaves—virtually all of them living in the southern states. Throughout that decade and into the next, the South continued to rely on agriculture as the basis of its economy; the North,

An antislavery meeting takes place in Boston as the abolition movement gains strength in the mid–1800s.

which became ever more industrialized, experienced enormous population growth.

BROKEN DREAMS AND NEW OPPORTUNITIES

One of Garfield's favorite activities as a boy was reading. He particularly enjoyed tales of great seafarers who sailed around the world on exciting adventures. He was so taken with these stories, in fact, that he left home at the age of sixteen and headed for the city of Cleveland. He hoped to get a job on the high seas but had to settle for canal work along the shores of nearby Lake Erie. The scene he discovered at Lake Erie—slow-moving canal barges pulling up to docks where brawny laborers scraped out a meager living hauling cargo all day long—was very different from the one he had imagined.

Undaunted, Garfield decided to give this life a try. It did not take long for his colleagues to notice that he was a hard worker—but it also did not take long for some of the more unsavory characters in this rough-and-tumble world to take a disliking to him for being so young and straitlaced. More than once he had to defend himself with his fists. While he turned out to be a respectable fighter, he realized waterfront work bore little resemblance to the romantic escapades of the characters in his books. When he contracted malaria in October 1848, he decided to return home. James's mother, who had disapproved of her son's venture in the first place, cared for him until he returned to full health a few months later.

At age of just sixteen, Garfield moved away from home and took a job working among the canal boats on the shores of Lake Erie.

During his recovery, James began talking about taking another shot at his dream of life on the high seas as soon as he felt well again. His mother suggested he think about getting an education first, and James agreed. In March 1849 he arrived at the Geauga Academy, located in the nearby town of Chester, with seventeen dollars in his pocket—money given to him by his mother and his brother Thomas. Geauga had about 150 students at the time, all from surrounding towns and villages.

James's subjects at Geauga included reading, grammar, and arithmetic, plus some history and philosophy. One of his favorite subjects was ancient languages. He also delighted in the art of debate—formal argumentation on a particular issue. His beliefs were strong, and he was not afraid to speak his mind when he felt he was right about something. He had a good speaking voice, a persuasive manner, and a natural flair for **oration**. As a result, he won more debates than he lost.

Garfield's future wife, Lucretia Rudolph, was a Geauga student at this time. Lucretia was a quiet and serious individual who focused on her schoolwork, and James, with little experience around girls, was initially too shy to approach her.

In 1851 James enrolled at a school run by the Disciples of Christ—the Western Reserve Eclectic Institute, located in the town of Hiram. When he arrived there in August, he was somewhat surprised to find it was nothing more than a brick building in the middle of a cornfield surrounded by smaller structures that served as housing for the students. The institute was little known and poorly financed, but James overlooked these considerations because he was impressed by the school's academic depth. He stated, "A few days after the beginning of the term, I saw a class of three reciting in mathematics—geometry, I think. I had never seen a geometry, and, regarding both teacher and class with a feeling of reverential awe for the intellectual height to which they had climbed, I studied their faces so closely that I seem to see them now as distinctly as I saw them then."

James dove into the learning experience at the institute and absorbed all the information he could; his love of books served him well during this period. His studies included literature, geology, trigonometry, and penmanship. He also continued honing his skills as a speaker and debater, and by the end of his first term, he was elected to deliver the school's valedictory address. He used his speaking skills outside school as well—in the spring of 1853, he began giving sermons on behalf of the Disciples of Christ. He was soon preaching once a week and being paid for his services.

By his second term at the Eclectic, he had so impressed his instructors that he was entrusted to give lessons to younger students. He also took the first steps toward forming a bond with Lucretia Rudolph, whom he had admired at Geauga. Although he still found her somewhat distant and withdrawn, he sensed a soft inner nature. He soon discovered that he was correct in his assumptions, and that she was also attracted to him. Thus began a relationship that would last until his death.

An Uncertain Future for All

The United States continued to expand geographically; it gained Texas from Mexico in 1845 and acquired California in 1850. With expansion the issue of slavery—which new states would support it, which would not—became increasingly tense. The South became ever more stubborn, insisting that African slaves were inherently inferior beings and therefore had no

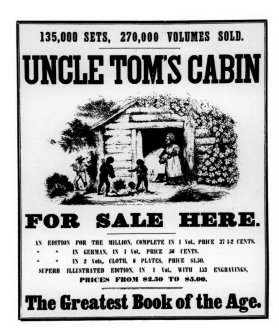

A poster from 1852 advertises Harriet Beecher Stowe's antislavery novel Uncle Tom's Cabin.

need to elevate their position in society. Meanwhile, abolitionist numbers continued to grow.

In June 1851 the magazine *National Era* began publishing serialized installments of a new novel by a white abolitionist named Harriet Beecher Stowe. Titled *Uncle Tom's Cabin*, it gave Americans a vivid view of the often brutal institution of slavery in the South by lifting the veil on the suffering many slaves endured at the hands of their masters. Southerners argued that the book's portrayal of their culture was distorted, whereas northern abolitionists used it as evidence to support their cause.

Political leaders tried to hold the nation together by finding points of compromise between the North and South. For a time they were successful. Then, in 1854, a Democratic senator from Illinois named Stephen Douglas proposed legislation known as the Kansas-Nebraska Act. Intended in part to secure the creation of a railroad through the region and into the emerging westward sprawl, it further inflamed sectional division. Part of the act involved a concept known as popular sovereignty, which gave new states the power to decide for themselves whether they would permit slavery or not. In Kansas Territory, this concept led to violent clashes between citizens. It also led to the creation of a new political party—the Republican Party, made

FIGHTING BACK

The abolition movement did not exist only in the United States—by 1830 slavery had already been outlawed in every South American country except Brazil, which outlawed it in 1888, and the British Empire had enacted the Abolition Act in 1833. Although the U.S. Constitution permitted slave owners to find and reclaim any slaves who had escaped, abolitionists joined together to help slave refugees escape into free states or into Canada, via the famous Underground Railroad, to begin life anew. When the abolition movement found its way into the slave states themselves, the realization that many people sympathized with them gave slaves hope for the future, greater courage, and even a sense of rebellion. Some rebelled by organizing revolts or strikes; others turned to more passive tactics, such as doing as little work as possible.

up of politicians from existing parties who had an antislavery stance. The **Democratic Party**, meanwhile, was splitting up over the slavery question, with those who opposed it joining the new Republican Party. With the presidential election of 1860 fast approaching, the nation was in desperate need of fresh leadership.

Changes were also in the making for Garfield in 1854. Although he had enjoyed his time at the Eclectic Institute, he decided to leave because he wanted to earn a degree, and the Eclectic Institute was not accredited to award them. After contacting several different schools, he decided on Williams College, in Williamstown, Massachusetts, largely because of a letter he received from the college president, Mark Hopkins. Garfield said

Pro-slavery forces ferry Missourians to the Kansas shore to vote against abolotionist legislation.

at the time,

> *I therefore wrote to the President of Brown University, Yale, and Williams, setting forth the amount of study I had done, and asking how long it would take me to finish their course. Their answers are now before me. All tell me I can graduate in two years. They are all brief business notes, but President Hopkins concludes with this sentence: "If you come here, we shall be glad to do what we can for you." Other things being so nearly equal, this sentence, which seems to be a kind of friendly grasp of the hand, has settled the question for me. I shall start for Williams next week.*

Hopkins was a respected and accomplished figure at Williams. He had overseen a period of tremendous growth in faculty size, subjects taught, resource materials, and, in a larger sense, Williams's scholarly reputation. When Garfield began attending in September 1854, he and Hopkins quickly became friends and remained so throughout his time there.

With Hopkins acting as a guiding light, Garfield thrived in the nurturing, education-rich environment. He broadened his knowledge of ancient languages, continued to sharpen his speaking and debating skills, and became popular among his fellow students, some of whom became lifelong friends. As a former farm boy, he was initially concerned about how his classmates who came from more privileged backgrounds would treat him. He was, afterall, in the Northeast, where there was rapid industrial development and where many of the nation's wealthiest families lived. However, these worries were unfounded, for they accepted Garfield as one of their own.

Garfield graduated from Williams in August 1856 with a record of high academic achievement and excellent grades. His extracurricular accomplishments included being chief editor of the school's literary magazine, the *Williams Quarterly*, president of the literary club, and a member of the Theological Society. When he gave a speech on graduation day, President Hopkins looked on with great affection. Biographer Ira Rutkow wrote,

Hopkins, sitting in a high pulpit, leaned forward and listened as Garfield took command of the audience. According to one eyewitness, "pride and affection he might have felt for a son" filled Hopkins's eyes. At the conclusion, applause rocked the church and thrown bouquets littered the floor as a confident Garfield ended his college career.

With the United States of America teetering on the brink of unprecedented internal conflict, James Garfield was ready to go out and find his place in it.

From One Career to Another

After graduating from Williams, Garfield returned to Ohio and took a teaching position at the Eclectic Institute (now known as Hiram College), where he taught a range of subjects that included ancient languages, history, philosophy, literature, and mathematics. The fact that the Eclectic had progressed little since his time as a student there distressed Garfield. He felt the school's leadership had not done enough to advance the school's academic offerings, improve its facilities, or provide teaching methods that were inspiring to its students.

Garfield was offered the school's presidency within a year of his employment. He took the position although he had not been seeking it. In a letter to a friend he wrote, "I have been buffeting such waves as I have never before breasted, and doing such work as I never before have done. There has come a great crisis upon the Eclectic Institute . . . and yet I never by word or action manifested the least desire to gain the Presidency of the Eclectic." Nevertheless, given this task, he immediately began making changes. One of his aims was to focus more on the student than on the educational material, the goal being to make the learning experience more interesting and enjoyable. Soon the school's reputation began to improve, and more students enrolled.

On the personal front, Garfield had moved forward with his relationship with Lucretia Rudolph. After a long courtship, they were married in a quiet ceremony at Lucretia's home on November 11, 1858.

Garfield was soon feeling restless, with a sense that he had the potential to achieve greater things. The question, however, was in what area he could go about unleashing that potential. He considered the legal profession, as he had begun studying law and had a fondness for it. He also considered another profession, one that surprised him somewhat—politics. As a younger man, he had had little affection for the political process; the bickering, backstabbing, deal making, and corruption were too distasteful to consider politics as a profession. Having become more enlightened through his own education, he began to develop strong views on important issues of the day—issues to which he thought, through politics, he might be able to make a contribution.

James Garfield married Lucretia Rudolph in 1858. They went on to have seven children.

A New Career

Garfield began volunteering his services as a public speaker—his skills were improving in part because he was still preaching for the Disciples of Christ in his spare time—on behalf of the newly formed Republican Party. The Republicans' strongest position was on slavery—they were firmly against it, as was Garfield.

Slavery had existed in the United States in one form or another since the early 1600s, and there had always been an underlying desire among the abolitionists to see it ended. Now the abolition movement was beginning to develop momentum, and the creation of the Republican Party was only one of several organized efforts to address the issue. As a religious man, Garfield felt that enslaving another human being was a sin, and he was happy to have a platform upon which to speak out. He frequently backed up his words with actions; he once harbored a fugitive slave who was on his way to Canada—an action that could have landed him in trouble.

James Garfield's gift for public speaking played a major role in his success as a politician, starting with his election to the Ohio State Senate.

Through his impassioned speeches, his local image as a public figure grew quickly. Republican leaders in his home state began to notice the effect he was having on audiences, and they realized he was a valuable asset to their cause. In a move that benefited both the party and Garfield himself, he was elected to Ohio's state senate in October 1859, the youngest person ever to receive this privilege. While Garfield was pleased with the exciting new opportunity, his daily workload increased—as he retained his position at the Eclectic Institute and had to travel back and forth between the institute and Ohio's state capitol in Columbus.

He was particularly proud of the way he had acquired his position in the state senate, as a letter he wrote at the time shows.

Long ago, you know, I had thoughts of a public career, but I fully resolved to forego it all, unless it could be obtained without wading through the mire into which politicians usually plunge. The nomination was tendered me, and that by acclamation, though there were five candidates. I never solicited the place, nor did I make any bargain to secure it. I shall endeavor to do my duty, and if I never rise any higher, I hope to have the consolation that my manhood is unsullied by the past.

While Garfield was entering the world of politics, changes were also occurring around the United States. Minnesota and Oregon were formally admitted as states (in 1858 and 1859, respectively) as the nation's westward expansion continued. In Illinois, a Republican named Abraham Lincoln had lost his bid for a seat in the U.S. Senate in 1858 and was considering whether he wanted anything more to do with politics. In addition, the Republican Party was gaining favor among American citizens in the northern states, where antislavery sentiment had always been the strongest, owing largely to a much smaller dependence on agriculture than in the South and thus a much smaller dependence on slave labor.

In the same month that Garfield was elected to the Ohio senate, a man named John Brown brought the abolitionist cause to a new level. Brown believed the best way to fight slavery was through armed uprisings. Many Republicans feared this approach would give abolitionists a bad image. On October 16, 1859, Brown led a raid on an armory located in the Virginia town of Harpers Ferry. His accomplices were both black and white. His main objective was to use the captured weaponry to help slaves throughout the South escape their bondage. Instead, Brown and his men were surrounded, and many were either killed or wounded in the ensuing firefight. Brown survived and was sentenced and hanged. His actions gave proslavery people reason to argue that the abolition movement was overly violent and therefore should be feared and shunned.

Abolitionist John Brown and his forces stormed the Harpers Ferry armory to gain weapons in their fight against slavery. The raid was unsuccessful, however.

Garfield quietly admired John Brown's courage and sense of purpose. He did not say as much publicly but maintained his stance against slavery. Meanwhile, he concentrated on routine government issues such as taxation and public schooling. Hoping to determine if there were any valuable mineral deposits in Ohio that could be exploited, he also pushed for legislation supporting a geological survey of the state.

On July 3, 1860, Garfield and his wife welcomed their first child, a daughter, whom they named Eliza after Garfield's mother. Soon after she was she born, Garfield was off again on political business—to make a speech in response to growing rumors that several southern states were considering **seceding** from the Union. The main reason for these threats was that Abraham Lincoln, once seen by many as a political failure, had been nominated by the Republican Party as its candidate for the upcoming presidential election. If Lincoln won the presidency, Republicans believed, he would seek to end slavery throughout the nation. In turn, much of the South's agricultural economy would collapse.

Garfield did not believe secession would occur. As a firm antislavery politician, he was happy to support Lincoln's bid for the White House. He gave more than forty speeches on Lincoln's behalf. Between his speaking schedule, his duties as a state senator, and his presidency at the Eclectic Institute, he was stretching himself thin. He was also getting tremendous exposure as a public figure. His name was being splashed about in newspapers throughout Ohio, and with his oratorical skills reaching new heights, most of the journalists who wrote about him had good things to say.

THE GARFIELD CHILDREN

James and Lucretia Garfield had a total of seven children, five sons and two daughters. Two did not survive childhood—Eliza (b. 1860), whose nickname was Trot, developed diphtheria and died at the age of three, and Edward (b. 1874) succumbed to whooping cough just two months shy of his second birthday. The five surviving children had impressive lives. Harry (b. 1863) served as president of Williams College and also earned the Distinguished Service Medal at the end of World War I. James (b. 1865), who became a lawyer and a politician, oversaw many of the civil service reforms his father favored and also served as secretary of the interior under President Theodore Roosevelt.

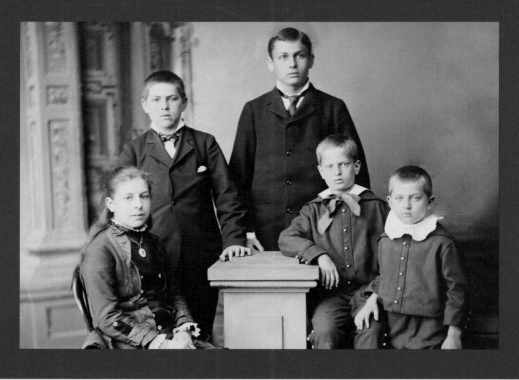

Mary (b. 1867), also known as Molly, became a highly educated woman for her time and eventually married her father's private secretary, Joseph Stanley-Brown. Irvin (b. 1870) earned a law degree from Williams College and was also involved in several charitable causes. Abram (b. 1872), much like his father, excelled academically and, following a passion for architecture, graduated from the prestigious Massachusetts Institute of Technology in 1896. Afterward, he began his own architecture firm in Ohio and also served on Theodore Roosevelt's National Council of Fine Arts and President Calvin Coolidge's National Fine Arts Commission some years later.

A Nation Divided

Lincoln won the presidential election on November 6, 1860. He received 180 electoral votes; his leading opponent, John Breckenridge, a Kentucky senator, received only 72. Just over a month later, on December 20, the state of South Carolina carried out its threat of secession and formally declared itself free of the rest of the nation. There was little doubt that other states would follow, and Republicans scrambled to offer proposals and compromises to avoid this.

Garfield considered secession to be nothing short of treason and was enraged by these developments. "To make the concessions demanded by the South would be hypocritical and sinful," he said at the time. "I am inclined to believe that the sin of slavery is one of which it may be said that 'without the shedding of blood there is no remission.' All that is left for us . . . is to arm and prepare to defend ourselves and the Federal Government."

He was so certain that war between northern and southern states was coming that he supported legislation to increase Ohio's military capabilities.

In the midst of this crisis, Garfield managed to broaden his professional horizons yet again. In early 1861, after having studied law for several years, he prepared to take the bar exam. The two men who were appointed to test him were political foes, one a Democrat and the other a Republican who did not agree with Garfield on many issues. Garfield went along with this arrangement because it would leave no doubt as to his expertise in legal matters. The two men made sure the exam was tough, yet Garfield passed without any trouble. He could now add lawyer to his growing list of qualifications.

Meanwhile, tensions between North and South continued to mount. As Lincoln prepared to head for Washington and begin his presidential administration, other southern states followed South Carolina out of the Union. Mississippi was first on January 9; Florida, Alabama, Georgia, and Louisiana seceded before the month was out. Shortly after Texas seceded on February 1, these states declared themselves a new nation—the Confederate States of America. They were also known simply as the Confederacy.

The Confederacy's constitution used the U.S. Constitution as a model but with greater emphasis on the rights of individual states (as opposed to those of the central government). It included a confirmation of the right to own slaves. The city of Montgomery, Alabama, was initially designated the Confederacy's capital. The Confederacy also appointed a temporary president, Jefferson Davis, until formal elections could be held. Davis was a veteran of the Mexican War, a former **cabinet** secretary under

The states that seceded from the Union prior to the Civil War are shown on the Banner of Secession.

president Franklin Pierce, and a senator from Mississippi until immediately after the state announced its secession. He did not favor the idea of secession, but he believed strongly that a state should have the right to secede.

Lincoln still hoped for a reconciliation with the seceding states, and in his inaugural address he tried to ease the fears of those who had already declared their independence from the Union.

> Apprehension seems to exist among the people of the Southern States that by the accession of a Republican Administration their property and their peace and personal security are to be endangered. There has never been any reasonable cause for such apprehension. . . . I declare that I have no purpose, directly or indirectly, to interfere with the institution of slavery in the States where it exists. I believe I have no lawful right to do so, and I have no inclination to do so. . . . We are not enemies, but friends. We must not be enemies. Though passion may have strained it must not break our bonds of affection.

Any hope of rekindling that affection came to an abrupt end the following April.

THE CIVIL WAR BEGINS

On April 12, 1861, Confederate forces opened fire on Fort Sumter, which stood on an island in Charleston Harbor in South Carolina. Located in the heart of the growing Confederacy, it was a key strategic outpost for the North. The Confederate forces demanded its surrender and evacuation. When the occupying soldiers refused, an attack was launched that lasted nearly thirty-five hours. The following afternoon, the ragged and exhausted occupants of the fort surrendered and were taken prisoner and sent back north. In response to the Sumter attack, President Lincoln called for 75,000 volunteers, some to protect Washington, DC, others to head south and confront the growing rebellion.

While the battle of Fort Sumter may have been relatively small in scale, it marked the beginning of the Civil War and, in turn, forced other states to choose sides. In the following months, Virginia, North Carolina, Tennessee, and Arkansas joined the Confederacy. (The Virginia city of Richmond was designated the new Confederate capital during this time.)

The Confederate army attacks Fort Sumter in April 1861, launching the Civil War.

Missouri, Kentucky, and Maryland also threatened to secede, but neither they nor Delaware, another slave state, did so.

With forces in the North gearing up for battle, Garfield was eager to participate. He had great confidence in his ability to lead. He also believed he had a natural degree of military aptitude. When he offered his services to the governor of Ohio, he hoped to receive the rank of full colonel. Instead, he was told to stay in the state senate for the time being and continue supporting important legislation designed to prepare Ohio's troops for the forthcoming conflict. Garfield complied but continued pushing for a colonel's commission.

Finally, in June 1861 he was offered the rank of lieutenant colonel, one step lower than a colonel. An irritated Garfield declined. However, with his political interests growing and the Civil War heating up, he found it difficult to focus on his duties at the Eclectic and in the state senate. When the governor offered him the lieutenant colonel's position again in August, he took it. A few weeks later, he was granted the position of full colonel. Some people believed things were done this round-about way to give the governor political cover, since Garfield lacked military experience.

One of Colonel Garfield's first objectives was to recruit young men to act under his command. He found them at the Eclectic—young boys excited by the romantic prospect of war and inspired by Garfield in his impressive colonel's uniform. Within a week, he had recruited all the boys he needed, and the unit became known as the Forty-second Ohio Volunteers. They received their training first in the town of Hiram and then in a camp near Columbus. Four months later, in December 1861, the unit was sent to Louisville, Kentucky.

Garfield's first assignment was in the Big Sandy Valley region of the Cumberland Mountains. Confederate troops were in the area, trying to convince locals to take up arms and join their cause, and Garfield's objective was to drive them out. Garfield's men succeeded and had only a few casualties—three dead versus eleven on the Confederate side. Garfield was praised for his leadership by his commanding officer and, through glowing reports in the press, was seen as a hero back home. Ohio's governor—relieved that Garfield was turning out to be a success and, in turn, making the govenor look good for having commissioned him—awarded Garfield a promotion in March 1862 to brigadier general.

Colonel Garfield was promoted to brigadier general for his exceptional leadership during the Civil War.

Meanwhile, President Lincoln approved a plan for a naval blockade of all Southern ports to prevent the international shipment of goods to the Confederacy. This strategy was designed to strike at the heart of the Confederate economy. As a result, prices began to rise, and many crucial items became scarce. However, the Union suffered its share of defeats, too. In July 1861 a major **offensive** on Confederate forces in Virginia, known as the First Battle of Bull Run, had ended with Union troops being forced back to Washington. General George B. McClellan, Lincoln's chief military commander, also tried to penetrate deep into Virginia in the spring of 1862 but had to retreat due to fierce resistance by the Confederate forces led by General Robert E. Lee. The Second Battle of Bull Run, fought at the end of August, resulted in yet another Union retreat and left thousands of Union soldiers dead or wounded.

CONGRESSMAN GARFIELD

With the war raging on all fronts, Garfield thought he could play a more important role if he returned to the political arena. This time he considered running for a seat in the U.S. Congress. Along with his many other accomplishments and experiences, Garfield was a general, a title he knew would go a long way in making him attractive to voters. He received many letters from friends and colleagues back home encouraging him to run.

When he was sent back to Ohio to recover from several health problems in August, Garfield began talking with leading Ohio Republicans about securing his party's nomination for a seat in the U.S. House of Representatives. Party leaders agreed that Garfield would make a good candidate, and he was given the nomination in September 1862. He was receiving glowing reviews in newspapers in the area. One journalist wrote,

> General Garfield, known as the "Praying Colonel," is the Republican nominee for Congress in the old Giddings District, Ohio. Colonel Garfield, when the war broke out, was President of Hiram College, in Ohio, and graduated from that as a Lieutenant-Colonel of the Forty-second Ohio Regiment. He has since been made successively a Colonel and Brigadier General, for bravery and ability displayed on the field.

On Election Day, he received nearly twice as many votes as his Democratic opponent.

As the Congress would not be in session until December of the following year (1863), Garfield went to Washington to await orders for further military duty. While there, he befriended a member of Lincoln's cabinet—Salmon P. Chase, the secretary of the treasury. Chase saw many of his own qualities in Garfield, such as strength, determination, and ambition, and admired the fact that Garfield, like himself, had come from humble beginnings. Garfield looked to Chase as a mentor, someone who could show him the Washington ropes. The two men also shared a growing dislike of Lincoln—Garfield felt by this point that the president was being too soft on the South militarily and that his good-hearted nature was turning him into a weak leader.

Whatever Garfield's concerns about Lincoln's war policies, he could not fault the huge step Lincoln took toward the elimination of slavery when he issued the Emancipation Proclamation on January 1, 1863. It was, in fact, the second of two parts; the first part, issued on September 22, 1862, stated that all slaves living in Confederate states that did not return to the Union by January 1, 1863, would henceforth be free citizens. On January 1, Lincoln issued the actual Proclamation, which granted freedom to slaves in Confederate states not under Union control. The Emancipation Proclamation also eliminated the possibility of France or Great Britain aiding the Confederacy because it formally declared that the Civil War was a battle for the freedom of slaves—a cause that both France and Great Britain supported.

Not long after the Emancipation Proclamation was issued, Garfield received his new military assignment. He was to work under Major General William S. Rosecrans, a West Point graduate and, like Garfield, an Ohio native. Rosecrans was organizing a new army in Tennessee and needed field commanders and a chief of staff. He offered Garfield either position, and Garfield

The Thirteenth Amendment

The Emancipation Proclamation granted freedom to more than 3 million slaves in the Confederacy, but it did not actually abolish slavery anywhere in the United States. Slavery did not end until December 1865 with the ratification of the Thirteenth Amendment to the Constitution. This amendment—the first one added to the Constitution in more than sixty years—began with a proposal by a Republican congressman, James Mitchell Ashley of Ohio, in December 1863. Along with President Lincoln and most other antislavery politicians, he was concerned that the Emancipation Proclamation was no more than a temporary measure, only valid for the duration of the war. Thus, they moved to draft an amendment to eliminate slavery altogether. The Senate passed the amendment by a vote of 38 to 6 in April 1864, but the House did not do the same until January 1865 (by a vote of 119 to 56). The wording of Section 1 is brief and to the point: "Neither slavery nor involuntary servitude, except as a punishment for crime whereof the party shall have been duly convicted, shall exist within the United States, or any place subject to their jurisdiction."

took the latter largely because it would involve playing a role in making strategic and tactical decisions.

Union forces won some key victories during 1863. In late spring, under the command of General Ulysses S. Grant, Union soldiers captured the Confederate city of Vicksburg, Mississippi, and, more important, key locations along the Mississippi River. After moving on to Port Hudson, Louisiana, they regained full control of the Mississippi River and divided the Confederate army in two. In July, General George Meade stopped Confederate forces in Gettysburg, Pennsylvania, from moving farther north in what was the costliest battle of the war in terms of human life— roughly 46,000 dead, wounded, or missing. In November, Union troops, again under Grant's leadership, defeated their Confederate opponents in Chattanooga, Tennessee, and gained control of the state. Grant was soon appointed commander of all Union armies.

Garfield's military experiences with General Rosecrans during 1863 ran both hot and cold. He genuinely liked and admired the general on a personal level, but Rosecrans's occasional habit of hesitating instead of acting aggressively irritated him. Toward the end of June, Rosecrans led his men to drive Confederate forces out of central Tennessee. Garfield took part in this crucial campaign and found Rosecrans's leadership nothing short of brilliant. However, Rosecrans failed to follow up with greater strikes on the weakened and scattered Confederate forces. Garfield believed that a precious opportunity had been lost, and he said as much in private letters to Secretary Chase. Those letters were eventually leaked to the public, and Rosecrans's leadership was severely weakened.

In September, Rosecrans led Garfield and the rest of his troops into the Battle of Chickamauga, along the border of Tennessee and Georgia. With poor communications, waning supplies, and faulty intelligence information, Rosecrans's troops were soundly defeated. Garfield was unharmed, but several men close to him were killed. Soon thereafter, President Lincoln relieved Rosecrans of his command. Many believed that Garfield's letter to Chase played a role in this dismissal and that Garfield and

General Rosecrans led troops into the Battle of Chickamauga. Garfield escaped unharmed.

Rosecrans had become enemies. In truth, Garfield had served him loyally and faithfully, and Rosecrans wrote a glowing final review of Garfield at the end of his service. Returning to Washington in October, Garfield received one last promotion—to major general—before resigning his commission to begin his career in the House of Representatives.

REPRESENTATIVE GARFIELD

Garfield immersed himself enthusiastically in his new job and quickly figured out how to get things done in the House of Representatives. He discovered, for example, that his strong speaking voice was an advantage in the noisy House chamber. He also realized that having a powerful ally in Salmon Chase went a long way toward moving legislation forward. Chase introduced Garfield to many other important people, and Garfield made a few friends on his own. Reactions to Garfield's youthful exuberance varied—while some veteran House members found it amusing, others found it irritating. Similarly, Garfield's passion for debate occasionally got him into trouble, as he would sometimes oppose even members of his own party on important matters. He was usually forgiven for these transgressions, however, since he was a newcomer and still had much to learn.

Garfield considered himself a **radical** Republican. He took an unwavering, hard-line stance against slavery, and he did not look favorably on the Southern states that had seceded from the Union. He argued for equal pay for African American soldiers fighting for the Union, particularly those who had been free men when they enlisted. He also opposed the policy that permitted citizens to buy their way out of military service, as he felt it was unfair to those who could not afford such a privilege.

The Tide Turns

Garfield and his fellow radicals continued to be frustrated by Lincoln. Garfield was irritated by the president's refusal to support a policy declaring that all land in Confederate states be considered the legal property of the Union; he believed the states had forfeited their property rights when they seceded. In addition, he still was not convinced of Lincoln's willingness to be more aggressive in the war itself. "Not by smiles, but by thundering volleys, must this rebellion be met, and by such means alone," he told his fellow congressmen. "This is an abolition war. They [the army] have been where they have seen [slavery's] malevolence, its baleful effects upon the country and the Union, and they demand that it shall be swept away." When Lincoln sought renomination during the Republican Convention in Baltimore in June 1864, Garfield supported him only because he believed Lincoln had a good chance of being reelected.

One of the main reasons for Lincoln's popularity at this time was that the Union had begun gaining the advantage in the Civil War. Lincoln had appointed Ulysses S. Grant as commander of all Union forces, and Grant followed a ruthless, all-or-nothing philosophy designed to eradicate the enemy everywhere it stood. Knowing he had more men, was better equipped, and generally held more advantageous positions, he attacked both the Confederate forces and the whole of the civilian economy. His generals, attacking relentlessly from all sides, scorched farms and left entire cities in ruins. During the Overland Campaign in Virginia, which consisted of several battles in May and June of 1864, Grant lost many men to the Confederate forces led by General Robert E. Lee. However, Lee's forces

Ulysses S. Grant: A Lifetime of Struggle

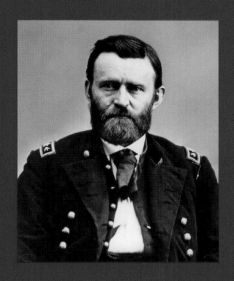

While Ulysses S. Grant's performance in the Civil War may have earned him the accolades of millions of Americans as well as a secure place in military history, his life before and after the war was one frequently marred by hardship, disappointment, and failure. Born in Ohio in 1822, he began attending the U.S. Military Academy at West Point in 1839, where he was an average student who, somewhat ironically, did not care for the structure of military life. Not long after his involvement in the Mexican War (1846–1848), he resigned from the army to spend more time with his wife and children and to find a more lucrative career. After a succession of failed endeavors as farmer, realtor, customs officer, and storekeeper, Grant returned to the military when the Civil War began. His eventual success as a general became legendary, and he was elected president in 1868 as a celebrated hero. He knew virtually nothing about politics, however, and surrounded himself with dishonest people who poisoned his administration through ineptitude and corruption. After leaving the White House, Grant made a series of bad investments that left him almost penniless. After being diagnosed with throat cancer, he began writing his memoirs to pay off his debts. He died shortly after completing his recollections. The book became a best seller and left his family fairly wealthy.

also suffered huge losses and had to abandon positions in valuable Confederate territory. In late July, a critical battle waged in and around the city of Atlanta resulted in Union occupation by early September. These victories drove voters to reelect Lincoln over his Democratic opponent, George B. McClellan (formerly one of Lincoln's top generals until Lincoln relieved him of command in November 1863), by a healthy electoral margin of 212 to 21. Garfield enjoyed a similar victory at this time; he was reelected to the House by a three-to-one margin over his Democratic challenger.

By January 1865, the Confederacy's situation was dire. Troops were running out of supplies, were being paid only occasionally, and suffered from exhaustion. With the prospect of victory shrinking away, many began to desert. President Jefferson Davis even considered arming slaves. In February, Davis suggested meeting with Lincoln to negotiate a peace agreement and bring an end to the fighting. However, he insisted that Lincoln and the rest of the Union recognize the Confederacy's independence. Lincoln refused, and the war continued—but not for long. Lee, with his forces dwindling and the Union slowly surrounding them, had little choice but to flee the Confederate capital of Richmond in early April. On April 9, Lee surrendered to Grant in Appomattox, Virginia, and the Civil War came to an end.

After the defeat of the Confederate states, Garfield was preparing to tend to postwar matters when he, along with the rest of the nation, was stunned by the news of Lincoln's assassination on April 14—just five days after Lee's surrender. The killer, an actor named John Wilkes Booth, shot Lincoln while he

The Civil War ended when General Lee (right) surrendered to General Grant in April 1865.

was attending a play at Ford's Theatre in Washington. In spite of Garfield's many criticisms of Lincoln, he was devastated. In a letter to his wife, he wrote, "My heart is so broken with our great national loss that I can hardly think or write or speak. I am sick at heart and feel it to be almost like sacrilege to talk of money or business now."

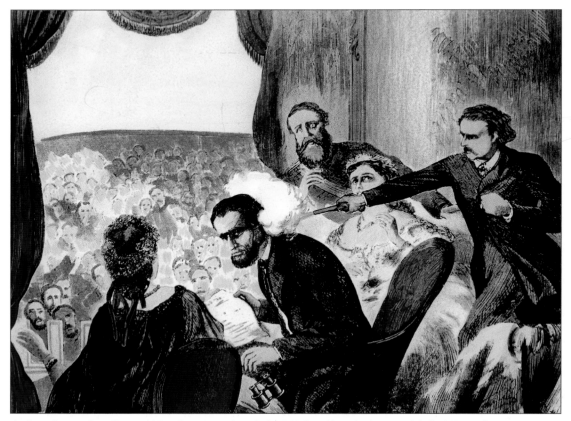

A few days after General Lee's surrender, John Wilkes Booth shot and killed President Abraham Lincoln.

THE RECONSTRUCTION ERA

The years immediately following the war, which would become known as the era of Reconstruction, required political leaders to focus on a number of pressing issues concerning the South and its citizenry. First, how would the former Confederate states be governed and represented in Congress? What would be the civil status of its former leaders? What were the legal rights of former slaves in the South who were now free?

To what extent would citizenship and civil rights be extended to them? Many leaders in the North had been discussing these points throughout the Civil War. Now the time had come to make decisions.

Andrew Johnson, formerly Lincoln's vice president but since elevated to the presidency after Lincoln's assassination, made several proposals. He offered pardons to all southern whites loyal to the Confederacy with a few exceptions (mostly those with political or military leadership positions and those with extreme wealth). He asked that each state organize a new government on its own and that they all abolish slavery before being readmitted into the Union. What Johnson failed to do was give former slaves the right to any meaningful participation in the Reconstruction process. Nevertheless, much of his plan began moving forward in the summer and fall of 1865.

Garfield disagreed with nearly all aspects of Johnson's plan. He was particularly displeased with Johnson's refusal to invest former slaves with legal or political power. The idea that the former Confederate states would not take proper care of these people struck Garfield as absurd. Most southerners were still unhappy that slaves had been freed; they were not eager to have their former slaves play a role in civic affairs. As Garfield expected, violence against African Americans increased sharply, with about five thousand randomly murdered in the years immediately following the Civil War. The Ku Klux Klan, a secret society that advocated white supremacy, was formed in Tennessee with the goal of spreading terror among African American communities throughout the South. Klansmen also attacked whites who showed any sympathy toward African Americans.

In March 1867 Garfield supported the passage of the Reconstruction Acts, a bundle of **statutes** designed largely to override the Johnson plan. The most important aspects as far as freed slaves were concerned involved giving them the right to vote and the requirement of former Confederate states to ratify the Fourteenth Amendment to the Constitution before being allowed to rejoin the Union. The Fourteenth Amendment broadened the definition of U.S. citizenship to include former slaves and protected their civil rights under the equal-protection clause. President Johnson tried to veto the Reconstruction Acts, but Congress, with its large Republican majority, easily overrode the veto. Garfield considered this a significant victory not just for his party but for freed slaves throughout the nation. He also continued to have serious reservations about the state of mind of President Johnson. Garfield's biographer Allan Peskin wrote,

By April, Garfield was half-convinced that the president was either "crazy or drunk." . . . By May, he was actively campaigning

THE IMPEACHMENT TRIAL OF ANDREW JOHNSON

The tensions between the radical faction of the Republican Party and President Andrew Johnson reached a boiling point in February 1868, when Johnson was formally **impeached** for what his accusers claimed to be a series of crimes against the Constitution. In particular, he had exceeded his authority in firing Edwin M. Stanton from his post of Secretary of War, an action that the radical Republicans considered a violation of the tenure of Office Act. The act stated that the president could not remove a person from high office without first getting approval from the Senate. Johnson had already tried, unsuccessfully, to veto the act, but the veto was defeated by the Senate and made into law. Johnson had had a stormy relationship with Stanton and wanted to replace him with Adjutant General Lorenzo Thomas. Johnson's impeachment trial (below), which was held in the Senate, began in early March and held the nation spellbound throughout most of the month. In the end, there were thirty-five votes in favor of removing him from power—one shy of the required two-thirds. In spite of the partisanship involved, seven Republican senators chose to take a stand against their party largely because of their disapproval of how the trial had been handled.

After the Civil War, African Americans experienced much violence and death at the hands of the Ku Klux Klan.

against the president. In a speech at Hagerstown, Maryland, he labeled the Democrats the party of secession and rebellion and linked President Johnson to their cause. Within less than six months, Garfield had moved from a well-wisher and confidant of the President's to an avowed enemy.

MONEY MAN

Through the rest of the 1860s and into the early 1870s, Garfield's influence in the House of Representatives began to grow. He chose to focus much of his attention during this period on governmental money matters, knowing that they would be crucial while the South continued to rebuild and the North became more industrialized. He was appointed a member of the Ways and Means Committee, which made decisions on tax policy. He secured this powerful post largely through the recommendation of his old friend Salmon Chase, who in 1864 had become the chief justice of the United States. In 1869 Garfield became the chairman of the Banking and Currency Committee, which oversaw the nation's financial industries, and in 1871 he became chairman of the Appropriations Committee. The latter was particularly important in that it decided how government money was spent.

Garfield had an aptitude for numbers and a good grasp of economics. He was a strong believer in fiscal responsibility in government, and he would not approve any measure that threatened the nation's financial stability. Some of the major issues he faced included the postwar status of **tariffs**, the reduction of debt incurred by the war, the dispersal of money to aid in the rebuilding of the South, and the value of paper money that had been issued during the war—money known as greenbacks—now that the war was over. Coins, being made of precious metals, held the value of those metals. Paper money, however, was backed only by the word of the government. Garfield and his colleagues had to determine whether the greenbacks should be gradually removed from circulation or backed by the same precious metals used in coin making.

A Trio of Scandals

If there was a downside to Garfield's involvement in monetary matters, it was that he was almost guaranteed to become embroiled in a scandal sooner or later. In fact, he got caught in not one but three.

The first, in 1872, involved shares of **stock** in a company called Crédit Mobilier that Garfield had received. Crédit Mobilier was a decoy company set up to distract attention from an actual company that had been hired by the government to build the Union Pacific Railroad but was being investigated for fraudulent billing and undeserved profits. The Crédit Mobilier stock had been given to several members of Congress, apparently as a kind of bribe to keep the investigation from going too far. When questioned, Garfield claimed he knew nothing about the scam, and since he received very few actual shares of Crédit Mobilier, he escaped the scandal with only minor damage to his reputation. Peskin wrote, "Did Garfield lie? Not exactly. Did he tell the truth? Not completely. Was he corrupted? Not really. Even Garfield's enemies never claimed that his involvement in the Crédit Mobilier affair influenced his behavior [as a politician]."

In March 1873 Garfield's name became linked to a second scandal, resulting from the passage of what became known as the Salary Grab Act. The primary purpose of the act was to increase the annual salaries of President Ulysses S. Grant and of all Supreme Court justices. However, Congress also hid provisions in the text giving its members 50-percent pay increases (and retroactively at that). Since Garfield was responsible for much of the government's spending, many enraged citizens put the blame squarely on him. The fact that thousands of Americans were struggling to make ends meet at the time added to public outrage. Although Congress reversed the increase, the damage was already done—mistrust among the masses was growing.

A third major scandal occurred in early 1874. Through his law practice, Garfield represented a company that was looking to secure a contract in Washington, DC, to build a series of sidewalks. He lobbied hard on behalf of the company, and when they received the contract, Garfield was given a substantial fee. Since Garfield was still part of the Appropriations Committee and had strong influence on government spending, many saw his involvement as a way of feathering his own nest; by making sure the company got the contract, he assured himself the fee. When the story reached the public, Garfield argued that much of the work he did for the company was in fact legal in nature; it did not involve the use of persuasion with his Appropriations colleagues to issue the contract. Garfield was never charged with breaking any laws, but his actions did little to disprove the notion that the Washington environment, under Republican control, had become tainted by corruption.

HELPING HAYES

The presidential election of 1876 became one of the most hotly contested and controversial in U.S. history. It was expected to be a close race, what with years of scandal shaking the public's confidence in the Republican Party while thousands of citizens were out of work. Since the Republicans had been the prevailing party up to that point, they received the blame for the nation's ills. The Democrats, sensing the first real opportunity since

Garfield wanted to see the Republicans maintain control of the White House. He therefore backed Rutherford B. Hayes (above) in the 1876 presidential elections.

before the Civil War to regain power, chose Samuel J. Tilden, the governor of New York, as their presidential candidate. Tilden had a reputation as a fighter of corruption. The Republicans chose Rutherford B. Hayes, a moderate with a good personal reputation, to oppose Tilden.

Garfield did not agree with Hayes on most political issues, but he still wanted the Republicans to keep control of the White House. Campaigning extensively on Hayes's behalf, he gave dozens of speeches not just in his home state of Ohio but throughout the Northeast. When the election was held on November 7, Tilden received 184 electoral votes to Hayes's 165—but 185 were required for a win. There were another 20 up for grabs, because both sides were claiming victories in the states of Florida, Louisiana, and South Carolina (plus, there was 1 electoral vote in question in Oregon).

A committee was formed to investigate the matter, and Garfield was a member. Democrats, outraged by Garfield's participation, believed that, as a devoted Republican, there was no way for him to judge the situation objectively. Nevertheless, Garfield was permitted to continue with his duties, and in the end Hayes was awarded the twenty remaining electoral votes and, in turn, the presidency. Afterward, Garfield moved about with the protection of a bodyguard for a short time, fearful that some Democratic operative might attack him.

In spite of Hayes's elevation to the presidency, Democrats made strong gains in other areas of government. They became the majority party in the House, for example, and as a result, Garfield's power there was greatly diminished. In spite of the fact that he was the ranking member of the minority party, Garfield felt it was time for another career change—a move to the

U.S. Senate. However, President Hayes asked him to remain in the House a while longer so that he would have an ally there.

Civil Service Reform

Garfield reluctantly agreed to stay in the House of Representatives on Hayes's behalf, but he soon regretted his decision—it was not long before the two men began taking opposite sides on major issues. One of the most significant was civil service reform. For many years, politicians had developed the habit of giving friends and supporters comfortable government jobs, even if those people were unqualified for them. This practice was known as the **spoils system**. It had begun in earnest during Andrew Jackson's administration (1829–1837) and reached its peak during the presidency of Ulysses S. Grant (1869–1877). By the time Hayes reached the White House, the public judged the spoils system to be yet another part of the growing corruption for which the Republicans were responsible, and they demanded change.

Garfield was a strong supporter of civil service reform and had some ideas on how it could be implemented. For example, he favored the idea that an applicant seeking a government position be required to take an exam to see if he or she had an aptitude for it. Politicians who depended on the spoils system as their base of power opposed this notion. Nevertheless, Garfield feared the Republican Party would continue losing voters and, in turn, any meaningful say in how the nation was governed if the system stayed in place.

Garfield also had personal reasons for getting behind the reform—he was constantly approached by people looking to take advantage of the spoils system. "I should favor the Civil Service [exam] if for no other reason [than] of getting partially rid of the

This Thomas Nast political cartoon satirized the spoils system that begun during the administration of Andrew Jackson (1829–1832).

enormous pressure for office," he once said. He also said that office seekers "infest every public place, and [they] meet you at every corner, and thrust their papers in your face as a highway-man would his pistol." Most were people who felt they deserved jobs simply because they had given Garfield their vote or had worked on one of his campaigns. He resented the amount of time and effort it took to deal with them.

MOVING ON

Garfield was also discouraged by the struggles of being part of the minority party in the House. He tired of the constant battle for every piece of legislation, particularly when much of it originated from Hayes's administration, which he did not support in the first place. Hayes's popularity with the public waned when he began winding down several Reconstruction measures. One of the most significant was the removal of federal troops from the South, who had been put there to assure that Reconstruction policies were being faithfully executed. As a result of their removal, the North's influence on the South diminished greatly.

With the stress taking a toll on Garfield's mental and physical health, he once again considered new career options. There was talk of running for governor of Ohio, a position he would likely attain with relative ease in light of his enduring popularity there. He also reconsidered the notion of seeking a seat in the U.S. Senate. One happened to be opening up, and leading figures in the Ohio legislature, which was under Republican control at the time, let Garfield know they would be willing to give him the post. Garfield accepted, and he looked forward to beginning his new duties at the start of the next senatorial session in March 1881.

THE DARK HORSE Four

$\mathcal{G}$arfield had kept the idea of running for the presidency in the back of his mind for many years. Although he did not admit to this ambition publicly, he had written about it in his journals and discussed it with Lucretia. He had also been encouraged by friends and colleagues, as well as many of his faithful supporters back in Ohio, to seriously consider it. In spite of the financial scandals in the late 1870s, his reputation was still solid.

A NEW AGE, A NEW LEADER

The United States was experiencing huge changes at this time. Morality and ethics had become important issues to many citizens following the long period of questionable behavior by the Republican-controlled government. Religious groups formed across the nation and preached the gospel of clean living. Industrial production continued to grow, and U.S. factories churned out new products at an amazing rate. The heads of these industries began to amass wealth on a formerly unimagined scale. In turn, workers began to demand better pay, safer working conditions, and fewer hours on the job. A labor leader named Uriah Stephens said in 1879, "A plain demand upon employees for an increase of hours of labor shows what may be expected in this country; and they give us timely warning of the struggle and fierce opposition to be encountered before eight hours can be firmly established by statute law in the various States. . . ." Several organized **strikes** sent the message that workers knew their value and intended to be treated fairly. Women also began growing restless under the restrictions society placed on them. Wanting a say in government, they lobbied for the right to vote,

As the United States became more industrialized in the second half of the nineteenth century, more workers demanded fair treatment by their employers. It characterized a period of change that was taking place during the 1880 presidential election.

starting with a proposed amendment to the Constitution in 1878. The latter half of the decade also saw the invention of the telephone as well as Thomas Edison's patent for the incandescent lightbulb, two technological achievements that would redefine the way people lived.

Garfield realized the tremendous responsibility of becoming president during such a historic period. Leading up to the election of 1880, there were three candidates for the Republication nomination—Ulysses S. Grant, a former president; James Blaine, a longtime member of the House of Representatives who

IN THE AGE BEFORE THE TWENTY-SECOND AMENDMENT

At the Republican convention prior to the 1880 presidential election, Ulysses S. Grant hoped to secure the nomination for a third term in office. There were no term limits for the presidency at the time; the Twenty-second Amendment to the Constitution, which limits the president to a maximum of two full terms (consecutive or nonconsecutive), had not yet been created. Prior to 1880, no president or former president had sought a third term, in conformity with an unwritten rule begun by the country's first president, George Washington, who, after serving two terms, made it clear that he would not seek a third.

Grant was the first president to break this rule. After Grant, only one president actually ran for more than two terms and was successfully elected—Franklin D. Roosevelt, who won not three but four consecutive elections. After Roosevelt's death in 1945, Congress passed the Twenty-second Amendment midway through the administration of Roosevelt's successor, Harry S. Truman. It was ratified in February 1951.

was on good terms with Garfield although they occasionally clashed on political issues; and John Sherman, another political veteran who was at the time Secretary of the Treasury in the Hayes administration.

Knowing he was expected to support one of them, Garfield got behind Sherman. In truth, he did not think Sherman had much chance of receiving the nomination. However, he did not want either Grant or Blaine to get it. Garfield feared that with Grant's dismal presidential history, marred by scandal and uninspiring leadership, if Grant succeeded in becoming the candidate, the Democrats would win back the White House for the first time since James Buchanan's administration prior to the Civil War. As for Blaine, he and Blaine had disagreed on too many issues for there to be any alliance there. Garfield figured that by supporting Sherman, he could at least diminish the odds of Grant's return.

Garfield's marked disapproval of Grant symbolized a division in the Republican Party at this time. There were two main fac-tions, commonly referred to as the Stalwarts and the Half-Breeds. The Stalwarts favored the old way of conducting Republican business: keeping a tight rein on the South, returning to hard-line Reconstruction policies, and maintaining the spoils system. The Half-Breeds, on the other hand, accepted the fact that the public wanted civil service reform, and they showed a willingness to let the South begin governing itself again. In summary, many felt the Stalwarts had their heart set on the past, whereas the Half-Breeds looked to the future.

To keep Ulysses S. Grant and James Blaine out of the White House, Garfield supported John Sherman (above).

Garfield never declared himself a devout member of either faction, but he tended toward the Half-Breeds, since he wanted to push forward with civil service reform. What it came down to, again, was Grant—Garfield knew his renomination would be disastrous for the party. He decided to do everything in his power at the upcoming Republican National Convention—to be held in June 1880 in Chicago—to keep Grant from becoming the party's candidate.

Garfield's central opponent in this crusade was a senator from New York named Roscoe Conkling. Conkling was an elegant snob, opinionated and boorish, but he wielded a great amount of power in his state. He loved the spoils system and in fact relied on it as the very source of his influence—without the ability to promise jobs and other favors, he would have had few supporters. Conkling was determined to see Grant renominated.

THIRTY-SIX BALLOTS

During the convention, Garfield and Conkling implored the crowd to support their candidates. The first vote for the nomination took place on June 5, and Grant received the most votes with 304. Blaine was second with 284, and Sherman trailed with 93. While Grant's supporters may have been relieved that their candidate had the lead, they were still far shy of the 379 required for the nomination. Another vote had to be taken, and on the second ballot the result was almost identical. Vote after vote was cast, and at the end of the day, after nearly thirty ballots, there was still no clear winner. Many began to worry that the public would view the Republican Party as too divided to be given the White House.

When the convention reconvened the following day, the first five ballots ended in the same deadlock. Then, on the thirty-fourth, something unexpected happened—sixteen votes appeared for Garfield. They came from the Wisconsin delegation. Garfield immediately protested, as he had never submitted his name for such consideration. However, momentum began building in his favor. Many Republicans liked and respected him for his oratorical skills and political savvy. Perhaps more important, they began to think he was the right man to heal the wounds created by the rivalry between the Stalwarts and the Half-Breeds, someone who could rekindle a sense of party unity in the eyes of the American people.

On the next ballot, Garfield's vote count climbed from sixteen to fifty. Sherman realized his own chances of getting the nomination were all but gone. He even began feeling the heat from his colleagues. As Kenneth Ackerman wrote, "[Sherman] read the excited notes from Warner Bateman about the break to Garfield. From Pennsylvanian James Irwin he heard, 'You cannot be nominated. Give your influence to Garfield and save the Republican Party.' Sitting in his Treasury Department office . . . John Sherman understood that his future reputation could be colored by the dignity with which he bore his failure." He announced that he would give up his bid for the nomination and support Garfield.

In a surprising turn of events at the 1880 Republican National Convention, James Garfield became the candidate for president.

To the astonishment of many, Blaine did the same. Suddenly Garfield became the symbol of the fight to keep Grant from the presidency. On the thirty-sixth ballot, Garfield received 399 votes and, amid the deafening roar of the crowd, became the Republican candidate.

This Republican presidential campaign poster from 1880 shows Garfield and his running mate, Chester Arthur. Arthur was a lawyer from New York.

Conkling and many other Stalwarts were angered by this turn of events. To appease them, Garfield agreed to have a Stalwart join him on the Republican ticket as vice president. The man eventually chosen was Chester Alan Arthur, a New York lawyer and favorite political operative of Roscoe Conkling. Garfield barely knew him.

PRESIDENTIAL CAMPAIGN

Having earned his party's nomination, Garfield had to focus on earning the confidence of the American voters. His Democratic opponent was Winfield Hancock, a former Civil War general and hero. In the months ahead the Democrats spent less time building up Hancock's image and more time trying to tear down Garfield's. Worried about Garfield's ongoing reputation for integrity and honesty, they reminded the public of his financial scandals as well as the corruption that had become commonplace in Garfield's party in recent years.

Garfield gave more than sixty speeches that autumn, many from the porch of his Ohio home. Hundreds of people came to listen to these front-porch talks, which made headlines across the nation and were often reprinted in their entirety. Newspapers favoring the Democratic Party tried to find anything in Garfield's words that could be used against him, but he was too experienced in this area to make such mistakes. There was, however, one incident that at least caused some amusement; it was reported by one of Garfield's biographers:

> On one of these days, while Garfield was haranguing the latest pilgrims to his Mentor front porch, a high-pitched voice interrupted his speech with a yell: "Hurrah for Hancock!" Heads turned to see the embarrassed face of Garfield's own seven-year-old son Abram, who apparently thought it a cute prank before his mother whisked him away. Fortunately for Abram, his father could only laugh.

On Election Day, which took place on November 2, more than 9 million Americans went to the polls. The result was a clear indication of how divided the country had become on the issue of politics. Garfield won the popular count by less than two thousand votes—the smallest margin in history. In terms of electoral votes, however, he had earned a comfortable victory—214 to Hancock's 155. They both carried nineteen states—Garfield's in the North, Hancock's in the South. This outcome was proof that national wounds caused by the Civil War had yet to fully heal. It is also notable that Garfield's victory put him in a unique position: he was a member of the House of Representatives, a senator-elect, and a president-elect all at the same time.

THE GARFIELD ADMINISTRATION

Garfield was not naive about the many challenges he would face as president. He was aware that growing dissatisfaction among the working classes had reached a point where labor organizations were being assembled across the nation and within specific labor categories. The National Farmers' Alliance, for example,

Garfield won the presidency by the smallest margin of popular votes in history—less than two thousand out of a total of more than 9 million.

was formed in 1880 to draw more attention to the needs of the agricultural industry, which had begun to sag economically. Also, the 1880s would see the emergence of an aristocratic class in the United States, represented by families of great wealth, such as the Vanderbilts, Rockefellers, Carnegies, and Mellons. Through their considerable power and influence, Garfield knew, they would have an effect on many aspects of American society.

One of Garfield's first duties as president was to assemble his cabinet. In the spirit of civil service reform, he wanted to be certain he appointed people whose qualifications were beyond question. He knew many who fell into this category. However, he also wanted to be careful not to select only his friends and other supporters. Doing so would have the somewhat ironic effect of making it appear that he subscribed to the spoils system. Another concern was party unity—he wanted to assemble a cabinet that was representative of the entire Republican Party, not just the faction that he favored personally.

For Secretary of State, Garfield chose James Blaine. Although the two had sparred in the past on some issues, Garfield's feeling toward him was still generally positive. Blaine's support of Garfield had been crucial in securing him the presidential nomination. Also, as Garfield got to know Blaine better on a personal level, he began to like and trust him more.

The downside to appointing Blaine to such an important post was that it enraged Conkling and the rest of the Stalwarts. Conkling insisted that a Stalwart be given the other power position—that of secretary of the treasury. Garfield gave the idea thorough consideration. He was serious about making amends with the Stalwarts and restoring some degree of party unity, and so he gave serious thought to the secretary of treasury appointment for many weeks.

Garfield decided on William Windom, a senator from Minnesota. Since most of the nation's industrial power was centralized in the Northeast, Garfield wanted someone from outside that area in the interests of fairness to the rest of the nation. Windom had also been chairman of the Senate's Appropriations Committee and had proven himself capable of handling the government's finances. Windom was not a Stalwart, however, and Conkling was not pleased. Blaine also did not like the choice. Peskin wrote, ". . . it threw Blaine into a dither. 'He won't do at all,' Blaine flatly declared, insisting that Windom was incompetent. 'He is profoundly and absolutely ignorant of our finances except as Appropriations Bills teach—which is nothing and on the wrong side. Any fool . . . can spend money!'" In spite of Blaine's objections, Garfield stuck with his choice.

When Garfield proposed offering several lesser cabinet positions to various Stalwarts, Conkling took the offers as insults and turned them all down. In the end, Garfield put together a cabinet that was efficient and experienced and would hold up to public scrutiny. The grueling task took many months to complete, however, and drained Garfield of much energy.

GETTING DOWN TO BUSINESS

With the cabinet business out of the way, Garfield could focus on more pressing matters. One was a troubling domestic financial issue—the lingering debt from the Civil War. The interest on the debt alone was staggering, and Garfield asked Windom and his attorney general, Isaac Wayne MacVeagh, to get it under control. After consulting various financial experts, the two men found a way to cut the interest rate by nearly half and thus saved the government millions of dollars. Also on the domestic front, Garfield put Thomas Stanley Matthews—a lawyer, judge, and former Civil War lieutenant colonel—on the Supreme Court. Matthews was supportive of the pioneering humanitarian Clara Barton in her efforts to launch America's Red Cross organization.

Regarding foreign matters, Garfield was perhaps the first president to get a sense of America's growing power and influence beyond its own borders. With the massive industrial growth during what became known as the Gilded Age, he was correct in his assumptions the nation would likely become a global force and, in turn, a key player in international affairs. He looked on annexing the Hawaiian Islands, for example, as a possible extension of the nation's ongoing westward expansion. At the time, the islands were under the control of King Kamehameha V, and Garfield, along with Secretary of State James Blaine, was concerned that Kamehameha might form a trade partnership with European powers. To avoid this outcome, he and Blaine sent American diplomats to Hawaii to see if they could reach some kind of agreement.

The first major scandal to strike during the Garfield administration actually had little to do with Garfield and his cabinet, although it was exposed shortly after Garfield took office. It involved the delivery of mail in areas of the nation that were still largely undeveloped and therefore difficult to access. Such areas were known in the postal service as star routes because, on postal paperwork, they were often denoted with an asterisk (*), commonly called a star. Star routes were frequently handled by privately owned businesses that were contracted by the government. As it turned out, many of these businesses were overcharging

A Thomas Nast political cartoon satirizes the postmaster in charge during the Star Route scandal.

the government huge amounts of money for their services. When Garfield heard of this situation, he realized some high official probably knew about it and chose to ignore it. As it turned out, there were two guilty parties—and both had worked for Garfield's presidential campaign. Garfield had both men dismissed, and the billing for the star routes was immediately adjusted to more realistic numbers; thereafter, the government saved a small fortune.

Another dark cloud in Garfield's life was the persistently negative presence of Conkling. His ceaseless complaints that Garfield refused to give Stalwarts any real power within the administration were growing tiresome to the new president. In a gesture that may have been intended as a clear statement to Conkling that he, not Conkling, was in charge, Garfield appointed William Robertson, a New York state senator, as the new collector of customs for the Port of New York. Robertson was neither a Stalwart nor in any other way under Conkling's influence. While most citizens were not even aware of the collector's position, it was, in fact, very powerful because the great majority of commercial shipping activity in the nation occurred at the Port of New York.

Garfield knew full well that Conkling and the other Stalwarts would resent the move. In a letter to a friend, he wrote, "This brings on the contest at once and will settle the question whether the president is [the] registering clerk of the Senate or the Executive of the United States. Shall the principal port of entry in which more than 90% of all our customs duties are collected be under the control of the administration or [referring to Conkling] under the local control of a factional senator?"

Republican Roscoe Conkling was opposed to Garfield's opposition to giving Stalwarts too much power. In the end, Conkling resigned in protest.

Conkling eventually resigned his position and then tried to get reelected in a desperate attempt to reestablish his power base. This bizarre plan failed, however, and he never again held a public office. With the bitter contest between Conkling and the president over, Garfield—the clear winner—emerged as a man in control rather than one who was willing to be controlled. Garfield decided that this victory would set the tone for the rest of his presidency—a presidency that would not last long.

ASSASSINATION AND LEGACY

Garfield's victory over Conkling embittered many Stalwarts; one was Charles Guiteau. Born in Illinois in 1841, Guiteau was a lawyer by profession but had participated in few cases and was, in fact, not particularly proficient. He had also tried his hand as a newspaper publisher but failed in that endeavor as well. One of his greatest passions was politics, and he eventually became a devout Stalwart.

Charles Guiteau assassinated President Garfield in July 1881.

As such, he was a firm believer in the spoils system. He had written many letters to Garfield pleading for the president to grant positions to other Stalwart members. He was particularly upset by the Robertson appointment as customs collector. It was, Guiteau felt, the last in a long line of blows intended by Garfield to destroy the Stalwart faction of the Republican Party. Guiteau had also contacted Secretary of State James Blaine on several occasions to ask for a government position for himself. Although Blaine was polite in his responses, he always turned Guiteau down.

A Holy Mission

By late spring 1881, Guiteau's rage toward Garfield had reached the point of near madness. By June he was convinced that Garfield had to be removed from power and, in his mind, he believed it was God's will that he achieve this objective. He was so certain that this was a divine and holy mission, in fact, that he tried to make sure the gun he purchased was particularly elegant in appearance so it would make a handsome display item when it was later put in a museum exhibit in his honor.

It was not unusual at this time for the president to walk around Washington without bodyguards or other protection. He moved about like an ordinary citizen. It was also not unusual for people to stop by the White House to see the president without an appointment. Guiteau had been to the White House several

Where Was the Secret Service?

Although the Secret Service had been created in July 1865, it was not charged with the full-time security of the president until 1902, a year after the assassination of President William McKinley. The service's original role was to aid in the elimination of counterfeiting operations, which were widespread in the 1860s (currency was easy to copy at the time). In the years ahead, however, it was used to investigate other criminal matters as well. For most of its existence, the Secret Service has been part of the Department of the Treasury. In March 2003 it was moved to the Department of Homeland Security. It is not, as many people think, a government intelligence service.

times since Garfield took office, mostly to speak with Secretary Blaine in his attempts to secure a job for himself.

The lack of security around the president allowed Guiteau to follow Garfield around and carefully plan the shooting. After considering several other sites, he finally decided on the Baltimore and Potomac Railroad Station, on Sixth Street, which was not far from the White House. On a Saturday morning in mid-June, Guiteau was ready. He waited at the station for the president to appear, but when he saw Garfield's wife, Lucretia, still looking pale and fragile from a recent illness, Guiteau lost his nerve. He later said, "I went to the depot all prepared to remove him and had the revolver with me. I had all my papers nicely prepared. Mrs. Garfield got out and they walked through the ladies' room, and the presence of Mrs. Garfield deterred me from firing on him.

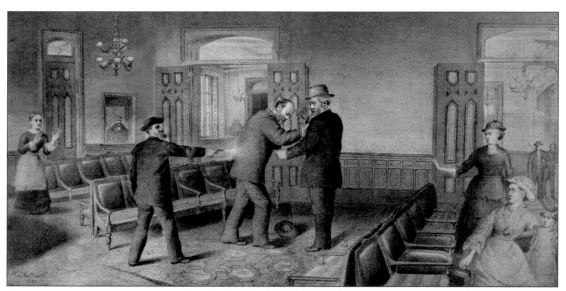

Garfield was shot by Guiteau at the Baltimore and Potomac train station, not far from the White House. Guiteau was apprehended by police immediately afterward.

[She] looked so thin and clung so tenderly to the President's arm that I did not have the heart to fire upon him." Guiteau withdrew and decided to wait until another time.

That time came on July 2. With Blaine and other members of his administration in tow, Garfield arrived at the station shortly after 9:00 a.m. to wait for a train to take him to Long Branch, New Jersey, for a brief vacation along the Atlantic coast. At around 9:30, Guiteau stepped within a few feet of Garfield and fired two shots—one caused a minor wound on the president's arm; the other lodged itself in his back. A shocked Garfield fell to the floor. Guiteau was quickly apprehended by a policeman who had been nearby. As Guiteau was taken away, he is reported to have said, "I did it. I will go to jail for it; Arthur is president, and I am a Stalwart."

Eighty Days

Garfield did not die immediately from his wounds. Doctors were quickly summoned and began probing the entry point in his back in a futile search to locate the bullet. In doing so, they were also infecting it with their unsterilized fingers. As Garfield came out of shock, he suggested that he be taken back to the White House. The doctors on the scene then covered the wound with an unsterile dressing.

In spite of the limited medical technology available at the time—there were no X-rays, blood transfusions, antibiotics, or intravenous fluids (all critical in the treatment of gunshot wounds)—Garfield began making a gradual recovery and, by the end of the day, was even in good spirits. Nevertheless, most of the doctors treating him believed the bullet had pierced his liver and thus did not expect him to live more than a few hours. When they were proven wrong, they changed their prognosis.

With the location of the bullet still a mystery, physicians suggested trying several different treatments. Since the doctors on the scene could not agree on exactly what the president's condition was, they argued among themselves. An additional reason for this hostility was that they were all competing to have their name connected with the feat of saving the president's life.

The doctor who was eventually put in charge of the case was Doctor Willard Bliss (whose first name was in fact Doctor). He seemed ideal for the situation since he had been a surgeon during the Civil War and had treated many gunshot wounds. However, Bliss made several critical mistakes in his approach to treating the president and kept more competent physicians at a distance. He seems to have wanted the spotlight to remain squarely on him.

Bliss decided the key to curing the president was to locate and remove the bullet. Having treated many gunshot wounds during the Civil War, he should have known better—it was not

An Inventor Lends a Hand

Alexander Graham Bell, best known for patenting the telephone in 1876 and for his work with the deaf, played a small role in the efforts to treat Garfield. Called to the White House by Bliss after being told of the president's condition, Bell brought along a new device he called an induction balance, which was actually a crude but workable metal detector. In spite of the fact that the detector had worked perfectly during tests in his laboratory, it was unable to locate the bullet in Garfield's body. Part of the reason for this failure was that Bliss directed Bell to search in the wrong place (in and around the liver, the place where Bliss believed the bullet to be). There was also another reason—the mattress upon which Garfield was lying had metal springs, which caused the detector to malfunction. Later Bell commented on his failure to help save the president's life: "I feel all the more mortified because I feel that I have really accomplished a great work and have devised an apparatus that will be of inestimable use in surgery, but this mistake will react against its introduction."

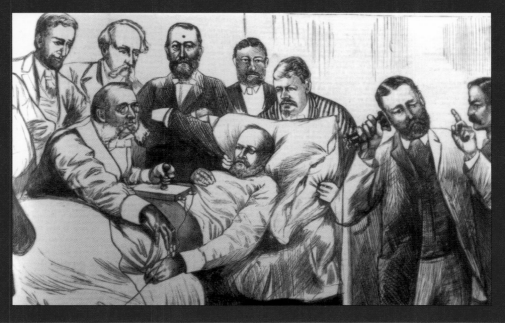

unusual at this time for a body to retain bullet fragments that had settled in relatively harmless places and survive. While he was considering treatment, an infection began to spread. As Garfield's condition steadily worsened, Bliss issued false reports of the president's recovery. Frustrated by Bliss's lack of progress, Garfield asked to be taken out of the White House and brought to the home of a friend along the New Jersey shore. He thought the fresh sea air might aid in his recovery.

On September 6, Garfield left the White House and began a railroad journey to the town of Elberon. A set of tracks had been laid from the Elberon station right to the door of his friend's home. All along the way, thousands of well-wishers lined up to watch the president's train go by; many threw flowers and straw on the tracks as a symbolic way of making the trip gentler for him. Bliss stayed at his side the whole time and continued to give news reports that many in the president's inner circle knew to be untrue.

In spite of the pleasant surroundings in Elberon, Garfield's condition continued to worsen. He died on the night of September 19, around 10:35 p.m., at the age of forty-nine.

AFTERMATH

The autopsy of the president's body revealed that the bullet had not, in fact, struck any vital organs but instead had lodged deep in his back. This discovery led many medical experts at the time to conclude that the bullet had not killed him; rather, poor medical treatment had. Garfield's body was later buried in Cleveland, in his home state of Ohio.

Charles Guiteau was formally charged with Garfield's death, found guilty, and hanged on June 30, 1882. He remained defiant

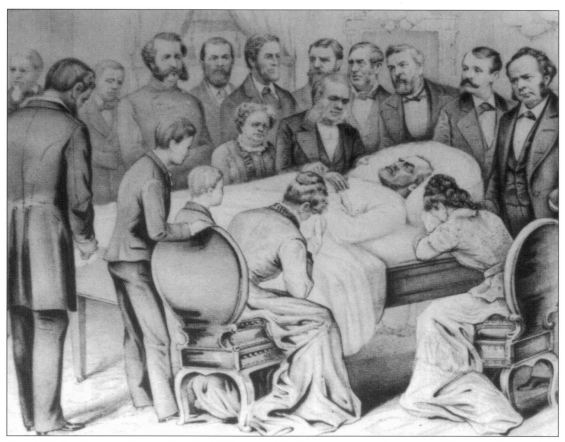

Garfield died late on September 19, 1881, probably due to poor medical care following Guiteau's shooting than from the wound itself.

until the end, saying at his execution, "I saved my party and my land, glory hallelujah!" Throughout his trial, he made no attempt to refute the accusation that he had fired the fatal bullet. However, he still did not take responsibility for the president's death—he insisted that he had indeed shot Garfield but that poor medical care had killed him. Bliss, whose reputation as a physician was never the same, continued to defend his treatment of the president until his own death in 1889.

Three days after Garfield's death, Vice President Chester Alan Arthur was sworn in to replace him. Many feared that, as a Stalwart, he would undo the plans Garfield had been making to advance the cause of civil service reform. Arthur surprised the political world when he worked to implement those reforms rather than remove them. He signed the Pendleton Civil Service Reform Act into law in January 1883. The act provided the first legal blow to the spoils system by creating a framework in which federal jobs could be obtained only through the merit system. It did not cover state and local jobs, but it was a start. Subsequent legislation through the years advanced this cause much further.

LEGACY

Since Garfield's presidency was so brief, much of it has been overlooked or forgotten. His death, which drew attention to civil service reform and to the shortcomings of emergency medical care, is the best-remembered thing about it. Yet James Abram Garfield was a decent and fair-minded man who fought for his principles. He labored to eliminate slavery in the United States and to secure the rights of those who had been forced to endure it.

He was passionate and ambitious, with a gift for oratory and a thirst for knowledge. He had been a politician, lawyer, preacher, soldier, teacher, father, and husband, and he had many other interests as well. He exemplifies a core component of the American dream: the belief that a person can start with nothing and, through hard work and determination, make it to the top.

Inspite of his brief presidency, James Garfield had a well-earned reputation as a man of fairness and decency.

1831
James A. Garfield is born
November 19 in Orange, Ohio

1849
Begins attending Geauga
Academy

1851
Begins attending Western
Reserve Eclectic Institute

1854
Begins attending Williams
College

1856
Returns to the Eclectic
first as a teacher, then
as president

1858
Marries Lucretia Rudolph

1830

1859
Is elected to the Ohio State Senate

1861
On passing the Ohio bar examination, formally becomes a lawyer; is also commissioned a lieutenant colonel in the army early in the Civil War

1862
Is elected to the U.S. House of Representatives

1863
Resigns his commission (with the rank of major general) to take his seat in the House

1880
Is elected first to the U.S. Senate and then to the presidency

1881
Is shot by Charles Guiteau, a disgruntled office seeker (July 2); dies at the age of forty-nine (September 19)

1890

NOTES

CHAPTER ONE

p. 10, ". . . was not an enthusiastic farmer, but he was an enthusiastic helper . . .": William Ralston Balch, *The Life of President Garfield* (New York: United States Book Company, 1881), p. 52.

p. 16, "A few days after the beginning of the term, I saw a class of three . . .": quoted in Balch, p. 79.

p. 20, ". . . wrote to the President of Yale University, Brown, and Williams, setting forth the amount of study I had done . . .": quoted in Balch, pp. 82–83.

p. 21, ". . . sitting in a high pulpit, leaned forward and listened . . .": quoted in Ira Rutkow, *James A. Garfield* (New York: Times Books, 2006), p. 9.

CHAPTER TWO

p. 22, ". . . have been buffeting such waves as I have never before breasted . . .": quoted in Corydon E. Fuller, *Reminiscences of James A. Garfield* (Cincinnati: Standard, 1887), p. 256.

p. 25, ". . . you know, I had thoughts of a public career, but I fully resolved to forgo it all . . .": quoted in Fuller, p. 286.

p. 29, ". . . make the concessions demanded by the South would be hypocritical . . .": Burke A. Hinsdale, ed., *The Works of James Abram Garfield* (Boston: James R. Osgood, 1882–1883), p. 134.

p. 32, ". . . seems to exist among the people of the Southern States . . .": Abraham Lincoln, *Selected Speeches and Writings* (New York: Vintage, 1992), p. 102.

p. 36, ". . . Garfield, known as the 'Praying Colonel,' is the Republican nominee . . .": quoted in Fuller, pp. 327–328.

CHAPTER THREE

p. 42, ". . . by smiles, but by thundering volleys must this rebellion be met . . .": Hinsdale, p. 229.

p. 46, ". . . heart is so broken with our great national loss . . .": John Shaw, ed., *Crete and James: Personal Letters of Lucretia and James Garfield* (East Lansing: Michigan State University Press, 1994), p. 218.

p. 50, ". . . April, Garfield was half-convinced that the president was either . . .": Allan Peskin, *Garfield* (Kent, OH: Kent State University Press, 1978), p. 259.

p. 52, ". . . Garfield lie? Not exactly. Did he tell the truth? Not completely. . . .": Peskin, p. 362.

p. 56, ". . . should favor the Civil Service if for no other reason . . .": Hinsdale, pp. 502–503.

CHAPTER FOUR

p. 58, ". . . plain demand upon employees for an increase of hours of labor . . .": Uriah Stephens, in Judith Freeman Clark, *America's Gilded Age: An Eyewitness History* (New York: Facts on File, 1992), p. 64.

p. 63, ". . . read excited notes from Warner Bateman about the break to Garfield . . .": Kenneth D. Ackerman, *Dark Horse: The Surprise Election and Political Murder of President James A. Garfield* (New York: Carroll and Graf, 2003), p. 111.

p. 65, ". . . one of these days, while Garfield was haranguing the latest pilgrims . . .": Ackerman, p. 216.

p. 68, ". . . it threw Blaine into a dither . . .": Peskin, p. 524.

p. 71, ". . . brings on the contest at once and will settle the question . . .": quoted in Theodore C. Smith, *The Life and Letters of James Abram Garfield* (New Haven, CT: Yale University Press, 1925), p. 1109.

CHAPTER FIVE

p. 74, ". . . went to the depot all prepared to remove him and had the revolver with me . . .": Charles Guiteau, in Charles E. Rosenberg, *The Trial of the Assassin Guiteau: Psychiatry and Law in the Gilded Age* (Chicago: University of Chicago Press, 1968), p. 224.

p. 75, ". . . did it. I will go to jail for it. . . .": Charles Guiteau, in Rosenberg, p. 4.

p. 77, ". . . feel all the more mortified because I feel that I have really accomplished a great work . . .": Alexander Graham Bell, in James C. Clark, *The Murder of James A. Garfield: The President's Last Days and the Trial and Execution of His Assassin* (Jefferson, NC: McFarland, 1994), p. 115.

p. 79, ". . . saved my party and my land . . .": Charles Guiteau, in Justus D. Doenecke, *The Presidencies of James A. Garfield and Chester A. Arthur* (Lawrence: University Press of Kansas, 1988), p. 96.

GLOSSARY

abolitionism the campaign to end chattel slavery in the United States

agrarian having to do with farmers or farming

cabinet a group of people appointed by the president of the United States to act as advisers on important matters

Democratic Party in Garfield's day, one of the two major political parties in the United States and the one whose members were sympathetic to populist influences and unsympathetic to the enlargement of the central government

economy the financial structure and activity of a nation

evangelism the program or practice of actively seeking converts to a particular religious belief

impeach to seek removal from office of a government official, usually for abuse of authority, criminal activity, or other forms of misconduct

legislature a government body whose purpose is to create, alter, or eliminate laws

offensive a military term for an attack, generally a carefully planned and coordinated one

oration a formal speech; the art or act of public speaking

radical one whose political views are considered extreme and potentially disruptive to the social fabric

Republican Party in Garfield's day, one of the two major political parties in the United States and the one unsympathetic to diffusion of governmental power and desirous of enlarging the scope of the central government

secede to withdraw from membership in or allegiance to an organization

spoils system a system of political patronage in which elected officials make appointments to government positions on the basis of personal friendship or party loyalty instead of merit or ability

statute a law

stock ownership in a company, normally in the form of shares, represented by documents known as stock certificates

strike an organized work stoppage at a place of employment

tariff the fee or tax assessed on imported (and sometimes exported) goods

Underground Railroad before the Civil War, a secret network of homes and forms of transport maintained by abolitionists to help slaves escape to the North or to Canada

veto in the United States, the power of the president to refuse to sign an act of Congress and thereby prevent the act from becoming law (Congress can override a veto with a two-thirds majority vote)

Further Information

Books

Marsico, Katie. *Reconstruction*. Vero Beach, FL: Rourke, 2009.

McNeese, Tim. *The Civil War Era, 1851–1865*. New York: Chelsea House, 2010.

Otfinoski, Steven. *Chester Arthur*. New York: Marshall Cavendish Benchmark, 2010.

Sheinkin, Steve. *Two Miserable Presidents: The Amazing, Terrible, and Totally True Story of the Civil War*. New York: Flash Point Books, 2009.

Stroud, Bettye. *The Reconstruction Era*. New York: Benchmark Books, 2006.

Websites

James A. Garfield National Historic Site

www.nps.gov/jaga/index.htm

An attractive, well-organized page for the James A. Garfield National Historic Site, maintained by the federal government. There are links to other pages with more information about Garfield's life and times.

James Garfield

www.whitehouse.gov/about/presidents/jamesgarfield

The official White House page for James Garfield.

James Garfield

www.usa-presidents.info/garfield.htm

A site with information on all American presidents. The Garfield page has good general information plus a brief biography.

BIBLIOGRAPHY

Ackerman, Kenneth D. *Dark Horse: The Surprise Election and Political Murder of President James A. Garfield*. New York: Carroll and Graf, 2003.

Balch, William Ralston. *The Life of President Garfield*. New York: United States Book Company, 1881.

Barker, Alan. *The Civil War in America*. Garden City, NY: Doubleday, 1961.

Clancy, Herbert J. *The Presidential Election of 1880*. Chicago: Loyola University Press, 1958.

Clark, James C. *The Murder of James A. Garfield: The President's Last Days and the Trial and Execution of His Assassin*. Jefferson, NC: McFarland, 1994.

Clark, Judith Freeman. *America's Gilded Age: An Eyewitness History*. New York: Facts on File, 1992.

Conwell, Russell H. *The Life, Speeches, and Public Services of James A. Garfield, Twentieth President of the United States*. Boston: B. B. Russell, 1881.

Doenecke, Justus D. *The Presidencies of James A. Garfield and Chester A. Arthur*. Lawrence: University Press of Kansas, 1988.

Dulles, Foster Rhea. *The United States since 1865*. Ann Arbor: University of Michigan Press, 1969.

Fuller, Corydon E. *Reminiscences of James A. Garfield*. Cincinnati: Standard, 1887.

Hinsdale, Burke A., ed. *The Works of James Abram Garfield*. Boston: James R. Osgood, 1882–1883.

Hoogenboom, Ari. *Outlawing the Spoils: A History of the Civil Service Reform Movement, 1865–1883*. Urbana: University of Illinois Press, 1961.

Kirchberger, Joe H. *The Civil War and Reconstruction: An Eyewitness History*. New York: Facts on File, 1991.

Lincoln, Abraham. *Selected Speeches and Writings*. New York: Vintage, 1992.

Microsoft Encarta, 2009 Premium Edition.

Peskin, Allan. *Garfield*. Kent, OH: Kent State University Press, 1978.

Quinn-Musgrove, Sandra L., and Sanford Kanter. *America's Royalty: All the Presidents' Children*. Westport, CT: Greenwood Press, 1995.

Rosenberg, Charles E. *The Trial of the Assassin Guiteau: Psychiatry and Law in the Gilded Age*. Chicago: University of Chicago Press, 1968.

Rutkow, Ira. *James A. Garfield*. New York: Times Books, 2006.

Shaw, John, ed. *Crete and James: Personal Letters of Lucretia and James Garfield*. East Lansing: Michigan State University Press, 1994.

Smith, Theodore C. *The Life and Letters of James Abram Garfield*. New Haven, CT: Yale University Press, 1925.

Taylor, John M. *Garfield of Ohio: The Available Man*. New York: Norton, 1970.

INDEX

Pages in **boldface** are illustrations.

INDEX

ABOUT THE AUTHOR

Wil Mara is the award-winning author of more than one hundred books. He has written both fiction and nonfiction for children and adults, including several other titles in Marshall Cavendish's Presidents and Their Times series. More information about his work can be found at www.wilmara.com.